DO YOU BELIEVE?
AREA 51

by Natalie Deniston

pogo

Ideas for Parents and Teachers

Pogo Books let children practice reading informational text while introducing them to nonfiction features such as headings, labels, sidebars, maps, and diagrams, as well as a table of contents, glossary, and index.

Carefully leveled text with a strong photo match offers early fluent readers the support they need to succeed.

Before Reading

- "Walk" through the book and point out the various nonfiction features. Ask the student what purpose each feature serves.
- Look at the glossary together. Read and discuss the words.

Read the Book

- Have the child read the book independently.
- Invite him or her to list questions that arise from reading.

After Reading

- Discuss the child's questions. Talk about how he or she might find answers to those questions.
- Prompt the child to think more. Ask: What do you think is inside Area 51?

Pogo Books are published by Jump!
5357 Penn Avenue South
Minneapolis, MN 55419
www.jumplibrary.com

Copyright © 2025 Jump! International copyright reserved in all countries. No part of this book may be reproduced in any form without written permission from the publisher.

Library of Congress Cataloging-in-Publication Data

Names: Deniston, Natalie, author.
Title: Area 51 / by Natalie Deniston.
Description: Minneapolis, MN: Jump!, Inc., [2025]
Series: Do you believe? | Includes index.
Audience: Ages 7-10
Identifiers: LCCN 2023054900 (print)
LCCN 2023054901 (ebook)
ISBN 9798892132183 (hardcover)
ISBN 9798892132190 (paperback)
ISBN 9798892132206 (ebook)
Subjects: LCSH: Unidentified flying objects—Sightings and encounters—Nevada—Rachel Region—Juvenile literature. | Extraterrestrial beings—Juvenile literature. Area 51 (Nev.)—Juvenile literature.
Classification: LCC TL789.5.N3 D46 2025 (print)
LCC TL789.5.N3 (ebook)
DDC 001.94209793/14—dc23/eng/20240109
LC record available at https://lccn.loc.gov/2023054900
LC ebook record available at https://lccn.loc.gov/2023054901

Editor: Jenna Gleisner
Designer: Emma Almgren-Bersie

Photo Credits: koya979/Shutterstock, cover (top); Marius Sipa Photography/Shutterstock, cover (bottom); simonbradfield/iStock, 1; Alizada Studios/Shutterstock, 3; David James Henry/Wikimedia, 4; CT757fan/iStock, 5; DigitalGlobe/ScapeWare3d/Getty, 6-7; Ryan Fletcher/Shutterstock, 8-9; Courtesy, Fort Worth Star-Telegram Photograph Collection, Special Collections, The University of Texas at Arlington Library, Arlington, Texas, 10; Cubschoenborn/Shutterstock, 11 (background); Marko Aliaksandr/Shutterstock, 11 (UFO); Doc Searls/Flickr, 12-13; Adam Gregor/Shutterstock, 14-15; NASA/DVIDS, 16; Cvijovic Zarko/Shutterstock, 17; Gene Blevins/ZUMA Press, Inc./Alamy, 18-19; Craig Vera/Shutterstock, 20-21; Chromatika Multimedia snc/Shutterstock, 23.

Printed in the United States of America at Corporate Graphics in North Mankato, Minnesota.

TABLE OF CONTENTS

CHAPTER 1
Desert Secrets..4

CHAPTER 2
What's Inside?..10

CHAPTER 3
Area 51 Today..16

QUICK FACTS & TOOLS
Timeline...22
Glossary...23
Index..24
To Learn More...24

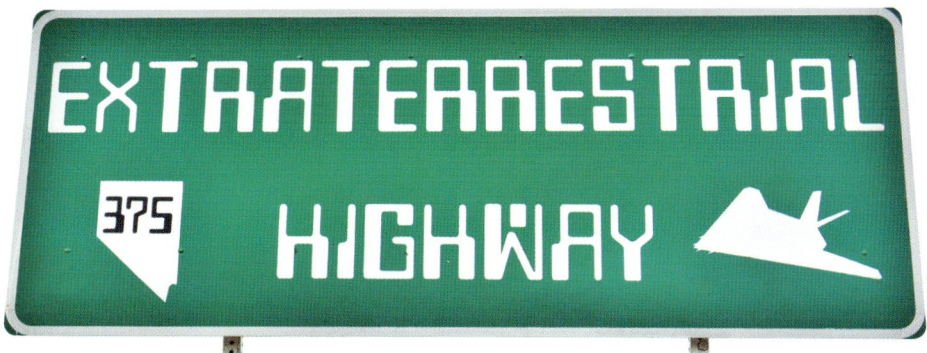

CHAPTER 1
DESERT SECRETS

There is a strange area in Nevada's Mojave Desert. Fences loom near a **salt flat** called Groom Lake. Signs warn people to stay away. Guards stop people from coming too close. What is this place?

It is a U.S. military site. It is part of the Nevada Test and Training Range. The U.S. Air Force trains here. It tests new aircraft. But this place is also home to the mysterious Area 51.

CHAPTER 1   5

Groom Lake

Area 51

What happens at Area 51 is **classified**. Only trusted military members know. But many people have **theories**. Some people think secret **inventions** are created here. Others think Area 51 holds **evidence** of **aliens**.

TAKE A LOOK!

Where is Area 51? Take a look!

CHAPTER 1　7

It is believed that more than 1,000 people work at Area 51. How do they get there? Many fly! They get on special airplanes near Las Vegas, Nevada. Only Area 51 workers are allowed on the planes.

DID YOU KNOW?

One U.S. government **agency** made a map of the United States. It broke the country into parts. Each part had a number. This part of Nevada was 51. That is how Area 51 got its name.

CHAPTER 1

CHAPTER 2
WHAT'S INSIDE?

Many people believe the U.S. government studies aliens at Area 51. Why? In 1947, something crashed near Roswell, New Mexico. People thought it was a **UFO**.

piece from Roswell crash

More and more people across the country saw UFOs. Many reports came from Nevada. There were machines flying over the desert. They did not look like any known airplane that existed at the time. Were they alien spaceships?

CHAPTER 2   11

In 1989, Bob Lazar came forward. He said he once worked at Area 51. Lazar claimed there were nine alien spaceships here. His job was to figure out how they worked. He said the government wanted to make more of them.

Later, people found out Lazar never worked at Area 51. But people were curious. What was going on at Area 51? The government claimed it didn't exist.

WHAT DO YOU THINK?

The U.S. military has many secret places. So do other countries. These are called **black sites**. Why might a military want secret places?

Stories spread. In the 1990s, more people came forward. They used to work at Area 51. They said the government used **chemicals** here. They did not get rid of them safely. Instead, the chemicals were burned. Workers got sick.

CHAPTER 3
AREA 51 TODAY

In 2013, the government said Area 51 was real. It was used to test secret aircraft. This is why so many people saw UFOs in the area.

The aircraft were used to spy on other countries. One was the **Soviet Union**.

CHAPTER 3   17

In 2019, a man named Matty Roberts posted a fake invitation online. For what? He invited people to **storm** Area 51. Together, they would look for aliens. People found it funny. Some people came to Rachel, Nevada. They held a festival instead.

WHAT DO YOU THINK?

Rachel is a small town near Area 51. It held an alien festival after Roberts' joke spread on the internet. People camped in the desert. There was music. Would you like to go?

CHAPTER 3

Area 51 still holds many secrets. Do you believe the government? Or do you think Area 51 holds proof of aliens?

CHAPTER 3

QUICK FACTS & TOOLS

TIMELINE

What is the history of the mystery of Area 51? Take a look!

1947
An object crashes near Roswell, New Mexico. People across the United States become interested in UFOs and aliens.

1955
The U.S. government begins testing spy planes at Area 51.

1989
Bob Lazar claims to have seen and worked on alien spaceships at Area 51.

2013
The U.S. government admits Area 51 exists.

JULY 1, 2019
Matty Roberts posts an invite on Facebook to storm Area 51 as a joke. Millions share the invite.

SEPTEMBER 20-22, 2019
About 1,500 people go to an alien-themed festival in Rachel, Nevada.

2024
Area 51 remains an active military base. What goes on inside is still classified.

GLOSSARY

agency: A group that provides a service for the government.

aliens: Creatures from other planets.

black sites: Military locations where secret projects or missions are done.

chemicals: Substances that cannot be broken down without changing into something else.

classified: Withheld from most people for security reasons.

evidence: Information that proves if something is true.

inventions: Things that are newly designed or created.

salt flat: An area of flat land in a desert, usually a dried lake or pond, that is covered in salt and other minerals.

Soviet Union: A former country of 15 republics that included Russia, Ukraine, and other nations of eastern Europe and northern Asia.

storm: To rush with force.

theories: Ideas or opinions that are based on some facts or evidence but are not proven.

UFO: Unidentified Flying Object. A UFO is any unknown object in the sky.

INDEX

aircraft 5, 8, 11, 16, 17
aliens 6, 10, 18, 21
black sites 12
chemicals 15
festival 18
Groom Lake 4
guards 4
inventions 6
Las Vegas, Nevada 7, 8
Lazar, Bob 12
Mojave Desert 4, 7
Nevada Test and Training Range 5
Rachel, Nevada 18
Roberts, Matty 18
Roswell, New Mexico 10
Soviet Union 17
spaceships 11, 12
theories 6
UFO 10, 11, 16
U.S. Air Force 5
U.S. government 8, 10, 12, 15, 16, 21
workers 8, 15

TO LEARN MORE

Finding more information is as easy as 1, 2, 3.
1. Go to www.factsurfer.com
2. Enter "Area51" into the search box.
3. Choose your book to see a list of websites.